Making Music with the Shakers

KEVIN HUGHES

ISBN: 979-8-234-06645-9

To my dear friends and bandmates, Nancy, Doug, Eric, and Dennis;

and to our faithful fans, who came to listen and dance

Contents

Acknowledgements

A special thanks to my friend and former bandmate, Nancy Howell, for stirring up memories of our time together in the Shakers. Nancy reminded me how we transitioned from playing mainstream rock and roll to more inventive, melodic, and dance-inspiring New Wave music. She also shared her perspectives on the joys and perils of singing and celebrity.

Thanks too, to Shakers guitarist, Doug Pierson, whose enthusiasm for my memoir fed my desire to tell a compelling story.

Much gratitude to copy editor, Lorien Megill, whose literary skills improved the continuity of my story and attended to my inventive punctuation. Her influence helped me make music jargon understandable to the non-musician.

Thanks once again to friend and graphic designer, Mario Ruiz, who converted old photo prints of the band into sharp, color-corrected images that amplified the subject matter. He also created an astonishingly good cover that captures the thrill of making music.

A heartfelt thank you to the many photographers who captured the energy of the Shakers on stage. We have made every effort to contact and credit all contributors for their permission to include these images in my book.

Much love to my beautiful life partner, Mary, who enjoys watching videos of the Shakers, but who regrets never having seen us perform. Thank you for your love and encouragement.

Finally, thanks to my son, Josh, who inspires me to write and to continue playing music.

Preface

Making Music with the Shakers is my love song to the days and nights I spent playing keyboards and rhythm guitar for the best New Wave cover band in Albuquerque, New Mexico. What set us apart from many other dance bands of the 1980s was that we didn't just play music; we put on a show for audiences that was as dynamic and fun as the music we played. Between 1980 and 1984, fans were just as likely to say to their friends, "let's go see the Shakers," as "let's go hear the Shakers."

While we mostly played in Albuquerque clubs, this narrative focuses on our touring days—principally because the road experience really exemplified who we were individually, and as a band.

This chronicle of our road gigs is based on a journal I kept at the time, supplemented by my memory—fallible as it may be—for the strange, humorous, and often wonderful things that happened to us as we performed at nightclubs and bars in cities and towns across the state.

While this is a work of nonfiction, I have taken literary license to embellish or amplify actual events, all with the intent of helping the reader experience what it's like to be a working musician, and enjoy a tale told with passion and good will.

To protect the privacy of individuals, I have changed the names of the establishments where we performed and the names of club owners for whom we worked. However, I did try to capture the behavioral nuances of the people in these stories. They were, without exception, memorable.

So, stepping around the guitar cases and amplifiers and drums, take a seat in our van as we travel to the Shakers' next tour stop.

Introducing the Band and Taking the Show on the Road

For me, being in a working rock band was like being married to four other people. The vows we'd taken were decidedly weighty, for each member relied on every other member to show up on time, make rehearsals, have the endurance to play three or four 45-minute sets a night, and keep other distractions—like second jobs needed to supplement a musician's income—at bay.

Like other Albuquerque bands, the Shakers sometimes had to hit the road to play in towns across the state or different regions of the U.S. to prosper in the music business. We met these new venues with anticipation and reservation in equal measure.

Playing in places where no one knew us or had even heard of us did have its benefits; we'd do all we could to dazzle club patrons with our music, our energy, and our stage show. When we were successful, we'd likely get a future booking; if the patrons didn't like what we played or the way we played it, we'd press on and set our sights on the next gig.

Over time, the Shakers got quite savvy at reading a club and its clientele. Business owners, bartenders, and wait staff typically asked us not to play too loud, so they could hear their customers' orders. Audiences, on the other hand, wanted to feel the beat as much as hear it. With the help of our sound engineer, we made sure the sound was full, without shattering windows or wine glasses.

The quality of the clubs and the clubs' lodgings for the band was another aspect of road gigs. We prayed that we hadn't been booked into any dangerous roadhouse dives or ramshackle living quarters where we'd be murdered in our sleep.

But the Shakers endured the hardships and undiscovered mysteries of the road because there was nothing we knew that compared to the thrill of playing music to a receptive audience. We were seasoned musicians who'd found a kind of organic chemistry that sometimes felt like magical realism.

I confess that there were moments when I wouldn't have been surprised to see Nancy, our lead singer, spin in her fiesta dress and hover over the dance floor as she held onto a high note for what felt like time slowed down—her red hair flaming like a beacon. Dancers often watched Nancy more than their partners for fear they would miss some nuance of her stage presence.

Beside her, there was Doug, looking like a young Paul Newman, playing a guitar solo that musically told a compelling story. Doug was all about economy. He never spoke unless he had something that needed to be said; he never plucked a note on his guitar unless it needed to be played.

Anchored to the beat, Eric would plant his feet on the stage, lean back, and hammer his bass guitar with astonishing precision. His eyes would dart left and then right expressing a warning of thrills to come.

There I stood half hidden behind three stacked synthesizers, making sounds like a piano, a harpsichord, an organ, a string or horn section, or a lone saxophone. Sometimes I'd get to start a song with a power riff like Bum-pa-da-bum-pah . . . Bum-pa-da-bum-pah dummmm.

Behind Eric, Dennis powered everything with his thundering drumbeats and nimble drum fills, his hair blowing rakishly from the fan at his feet. More than anyone in the band, Dennis could play any genre of music, be it funk, rhythm and blues, jazz, or hard rock—and do it well.

Nancy Howell - Vocals

Doug Pierson - Guitar

Eric Benjamin - Bass

Kevin Hughes - Keyboards

Dennis Painter - Drums

* * *

I never considered keeping a journal about the band until we took our show on the road. Before this, we had a lot of togetherness at home base, where we could gather during the day to learn new material, write and arrange an original song, or share what was going on in our lives. One tradition that emerged was for the Shakers to go to breakfast at 2:00 in the morning following our last set on Saturday nights. All-night restaurants catered to working musicians and their fan bases. It wasn't uncommon to meet members of rival bands, with whom we were polite but never effusive.

But once we hit the road, where we would essentially be untethered, I figured that we'd have some adventures and maybe some disasters, and the potential for drama was something I couldn't resist.

The Wild West

Aug 10–13, 1983
Ruby's Desert Restaurant and Bar, Los Lunas

One of the first stops on our road trip of New Mexico clubs and bars was a mere 20 miles south of Albuquerque, our base of operations. As we passed through Los Lunas on Old Route 66, we saw expansive acres of farmland with those giant irrigation systems that move slowly in a circle around a central water source. We didn't know what they were growing, but the vegetation was a rich color of green. Here too, we saw the occasional stockyard where cattle were clustered together, presumably soon to become beef.

Ruby's Desert Restaurant and Bar had been converted from an old adobe hacienda likely built in the late 1800s. It sat at a major intersection in the village and was a popular drinking and eating establishment, with a celebrated long bar.

The owner/manager was a big, imposing fellow named Ronny B, who was considered a good businessman and friend to the farmers, ranchers, railroad workers, and prison staff at the newly constructed correctional facility.

We started on a Wednesday night, and the clientele seemed to enjoy the music. Our soundman had a good mix, and we liked the acoustics of the room.

Several tunes into the second set, a waitress stepped up to the stage and handed Nancy a note.

"From the owner," was all she said.

Nancy read it, turned, and whispered with exaggerated silent expression, "The bar owner wants to see us, right away."

Nancy told the audience and handful of dancers that we had a technical problem we had to deal with and would be right back.

Ronny B stood by the long bar and motioned for us to come into his office.

Like a quintet of AWOL service members being corralled by MPs, the members of the band walked single file into the office. The space was actually quite impressive, with western paintings depicting cowboys on horseback wrangling cattle over the prairie; some beautiful Navajo blankets hanging on the walls; and a table lamp with a shade showing silhouettes of covered wagons, cowboys on horses, and saguaro cacti against a warm light.

"So, what I wanted to know was what is the music you're playin'?" he said. "It doesn't sound at all like the sampler cassette your manager gave me."

With the band standing in a semicircle around Ronny B's desk, Nancy spoke first,

"We're playing music that's current and right on point with what people want to hear. We follow Billboard's hit lists as our guide." (This was not always strictly true.)

"Huh," he said with disappointment. "I thought you'd be playing some Rolling Stones, that 'Stairway to Heaven' group, and maybe some Elvis and Paul Revere, and that fella, Lionel Richie."

Unconcerned that Ronny B described four distinct eras of popular music, Doug added, "Oh yeah, we can cover some of those tunes."

"That'd make me *real* happy," the bar owner said firmly.

Now we knew all those artists, but our repertoire was made up of New Wave covers of songs by—among others—the Pretenders, Joe Jackson, Blondie, the Eurythmics, and the Talking Heads. A cover band like the Shakers couldn't simply play any request out of thin air. "We aren't a wedding band," Nancy used to tell people. If folks needed more information, she'd say, "We don't play the 'Anniversary Waltz' followed by 'Proud Mary,' then 'Blue Moon.'"

Back on stage, we felt a bit shaken, but we started up the next song and continued to play the songs we always played. Two or three songs into the set, Ronny B stood at the bar and gave us a thumbs up. Nancy returned the gesture, and from that point on, everyone was happy.

On the third night of our four-night gig at Ruby's, we were getting ready to play our last song of the last set. For a brief moment, while Doug tuned his guitar, the stage was relatively quiet, and it was then that I noticed a high-frequency buzzing sound behind my right shoulder. When I turned to check it out, there appeared to be a wasp nest in the upper corner of the stage wall directly behind the band.

Nancy gave me that smile and look of expectation that I was ready to kick off the next tune—a song called "Don't Change," by INXS. Dennis (Denny) gave me a four count with his drumsticks, and I started the song.

With the dance floor packed, and even the bartenders and waitresses watching us, the song moved along famously. The energy was there and the band sounded tight. Then, halfway into the song, I realized that a giant wasp was orbiting my head slowly, trying to decipher who or what I was. After several bars, the wasp disappeared and I was able to turn my focus on my upcoming synthesizer solo.

A few notes into my solo, the wasp reappeared and became interested in my fingers, as they moved rapidly over the keyboard. I did what I could to flick the insect away, to no avail. Suddenly, my fingers played all the wrong notes in what felt like an incomprehensible bit of improvisation—all to keep the wasp from landing on and stinging one of my fingers.

After we finished the last song and Nancy wished everyone a good night, the lights came up in the bar and, setting his bass down, Eric stepped over to me and said with a smile and a soul handshake, "Man, you went way outside on that last solo!

"Yeah?" I returned weakly.

"It was sweet, dude!"

Nancy joined us and said, "Kevin, that was one of your best solos. I never heard you play it that way before."

The other notable thing that happened at Ruby's occurred on Saturday night, 20 minutes after we'd finished our last set. It must have been in the neighborhood of 1:15 a.m. when a bartender rang what sounded like a starting gate bell at a horserace, then shouted at the top of his lungs that this was "last call for alcohol!!"

Fifteen minutes later, he rang it multiple times and shouted, "Damas and caballeros, it's closing time! You don't have to go home, but you can't stay here!!"

At a quarter to 2:00, with barflies still finishing their drinks, we saw Ronny B come out of his office holding something in his right hand. One of the nicer members of the wait staff hastened up to the stage and said, "Hit the deck!"

Moments later, Ronny B fired a revolver at the ceiling with the report of a cannon. As blue gun smoke drifted through the air, lingerers got up quickly and headed for the door.

We quickly gathered our jackets, gig bags, and guitars and started to move toward the exit.

Ronny B, looking satisfied that his alarm had worked according to plan, approached us at the stage. "I hope you guys weren't thinking of leaving . . ." he said.

We froze.

"Without getting paid," he added, offering our check to no one in particular.

Doug stepped forward.

“Thanks, Ronny. I’m the band accountant; I’ll take it.”

Ronny B looked pleased. “You all can come in tomorrow before noon to load out your equipment. You guys did a good job. We had lots of compliments and good bar receipts. Plus, I appreciate that you played more of the songs I requested.”

Glancing at Nancy, Doug said, “We were happy to oblige.”

Airplane Adventure and Late-Night Guests

Aug 15–27, 1983
Trinity Bar and Grill, Alamogordo

Most of our engagements were booked for two weeks at each establishment. We'd play five or six nights a week, from eight or nine o'clock at night till twelve or one o'clock in the morning. What became a challenge was what to do during the day. As experienced musicians, we knew well the temptations that famous musicians often succumbed to, such as alcohol and drug abuse or tearing up hotel rooms. Fortunately, none of us ventured down those rabbit holes.

Days were routinely spent grocery shopping or finding good places to eat, doing laundry, and sometimes rehearsing new material at the band houses. On occasion, we'd take in local attractions like roller rinks, movie theaters, national parks, and such to pass the time. Scott, our soundman, often looked for amusement parks or go-kart tracks.

During the Trinity Bar and Grill gig, I convinced Doug and Denny to drive out to the Alamogordo-White Sands Regional Airport to see if we could watch some planes taking off or landing.

When we got there, the place looked deserted except for a boxy looking terminal, several hangars, some small private aircraft, and a helicopter ambulance. Denny then spotted two large twin-propeller aircraft sitting near the end of the runway. Since there were no fences or barriers and nary a sign warning us to keep out, we drove the van along the runway and parked by the two planes.

Each aircraft had a bubble-type glass canopy through which the pilots would have a clear view of the airspace. The nose of each plane also had a clear canopy, presumably designed for an observer of some kind. The planes' vertical tails bore the numbers 6 and 7, respectively.

As we stood beneath one wing feeling the wind ruffle our clothes and sweep dust over our shoes, we looked at each other and realized that our temptation to board the aircraft was far greater than the rational certainty that we could get into deep trouble.

Clambering our way inside one of the planes, we each looked for a cool place to investigate. Denny and I slid into the pilot seats in the cockpit. From there, we could look down at the giant propellers or look back toward the terminal, way off in the distance.

At first, we argued about who was pilot and who was co-pilot. Then, Denny started touching some of the gauges on the instrument panel, moving the U-shaped steering wheel, and pushing the rudder pedals on the floor.

“Denny, cool it!” I said, terrified he’d push, pull, or click something that would start the engines or retract the landing gear.

While I fretted about Denny, Doug sat in the nose of the plane puzzling over why there were no identifiable instruments for an airman to operate. Later on, we learned that the nose bubble was for visually tracking forest fires.

Doug later fessed up that he’d had a “let’s pretend” moment seated in his observation station, and yelled out—"German ME-109 at two o’clock; we’re taking fire!”

It was Doug too who saw an airport pickup truck advancing on us in a cloud of dust. Before the three of us could bail, several men stood looking up at Doug in the canopy and giving a friendly wave. I’m sure Doug thought, “Oh, s--t.”

Sensing our doom, we climbed down the ladder beneath the aircraft and shuffled toward the men.

Looking friendly with a toothy grin, the shortest man with the crewcut said, “We’ve been watching for you and thought maybe you got lost.”

Doug, looking somewhat perplexed, stammered, “You were wa-, watching for us?”

“Oh yeah.” Pointing toward the southwest, he laughed. “Some folks miss the turnoff to the airport and end up at White Sands.”

Doug continued cautiously, “How did you know we were coming?”

“Your manager, or at least someone from your office, scheduled your tour more than a month ago.” Nodding toward the aircraft, he continued, “What da ya think of our air tankers?”

Denny and I, looking pale and confused, took a step back as Doug asked Crewcut, “Who were you expecting—exactly?”

“Why, the video production company,” the man returned curtly. “You’re here to work on a promotional video for our firefighting business, our aircraft, our crews—right?”

Doug, the embodiment of calm, confessed to the men, “Gentlemen, we must apologize; we’re a rock band from out of town and are playing at the Trinity Bar. Our curiosity got the better of—”

Crewcut, no longer smiling, jumped in, “I hope you boys didn’t mess with anything. These aircraft have lots of delicate flight instruments and settings that shouldn’t be dicked with.”

"Are you shooting on three-quarter inch or Betacam?" I asked spontaneously.

"You boys know video, do you?"

Doug looked back at me and smiled, as if to say "you've got the ball, Kev."

"Oh yeah, we've made a music video and know a bit about the technology. You know, wide-angle lenses, three-point lighting, and stuff."

The airport men's blank expressions conveyed that they had no idea what I was talking about, but that was okay. Neither did I.

Still, this prompted a short discussion on the merits of video for marketing products and services. With little salient knowledge on the subject, we basically made it up as we went along.

A short time later, the two air tanker men asked us if we'd like to tour their facility, and we fielded a lot of their questions about being in the music business, like "is it an easy way to meet women?" They even said they'd try to come hear us Friday night, though they never showed up.

On our way back to the highway, we passed the real video crew in their van. Denny rolled the window down and yelled, "Hey, you're late!" to which the driver and passenger responded blankly.

* * *

Eric—God bless him—had an annoying habit of making friends at the bars in which we played and inviting them back to the band house after the gig. He was also prone to bidding his guests goodnight and heading off to bed with three or four hangers-on still sitting in our kitchen or living room.

One Friday night, more accurately, early Saturday morning, Eric invited a fellow and his two friends to join us in the double-wide mobile home we occupied in Alamogordo. The more confident friend, a stocky, curly-headed man, had brought along his own acoustic guitar, which he had strapped to his back like a quiver of arrows.

One may think us insensitive, but this scenario was usually a warning sign that we were in the presence of someone who was either a real musician or someone who desperately wanted to be one. In this instance, Barry—as his friends called him—told us that he was a prolific songwriter and had an original composition he thought would be perfect for our band to play.

Barry sat on the couch, took a pull on his can of lager, leaned forward with his guitar on his knee, opened a spiral notebook, and turned to a page of song lyrics, broken out into what looked like twenty verses.

Barry, not bothering to tune his guitar, began singing his anthem in a warbly voice. After ten or twenty repetitious verses, I excused myself and headed for the sack, where I was out like a light after a long night of work.

At one point, I awakened to an identifiable noise, stepped out of my bedroom, and heard Barry still singing the same song. Since Denny and Doug were still up, I let it go and went back to bed.

Moments later, I heard Nancy talking in the living room and got up once again to investigate.

Nancy, placing her cup of tea on the coffee table, said, "Barry . . . BARRY!" She stood in front of him and said in a kind but direct manner, "What makes us a band is that we write our own songs—songs that fit our genre of music and are a reflection of our own experiences. You may have written some good tunes, but you should seek out some open mic nights in local clubs, where you can play for people and get their feedback."

Barry set his guitar aside and sat waiting for Nancy to continue.

"It's late and we need to ask you and your friends to leave."

Nancy never ceased to amaze me. Not only could she deal with difficult situations that required tact, she could also do it with authority. I once saw her break up a fight between two guys who'd had too much to drink at one of our gigs. (I sometimes think she was influenced by an older brother, who at six foot four, could be an imposing figure.)

In the Pocket and Motown Moves

Sept 19–Oct 1, 1983
Sierra Mountain Lodge, Ruidoso

Not that anyone was keeping score, but I think my favorite gig on this tour was in the village of Ruidoso. Having left Alamogordo in the high desert, our tour road slowly climbed into the Sacramento Mountains to the northeast, which were graced with evergreen forests and charming communities like Ruidoso, Mescalero (of the Mescalero Apache Tribe), Cloudcroft, and Capitan—the birthplace of Smokey Bear.

Sierra Mountain Lodge and its accompanying roadhouse were nestled back into the woods and attracted travelers from all over the southwest who came to Ruidoso to ski, fish, ride horses, hike, and backpack. They also came to dance to live bands, which is where we came in.

* * *

On the Thursday night of our first week at the Sierra roadhouse, the Shakers were on fire. Drummer Denny and bass player Eric created a groove so deep, the dancers looked like their moves were choreographed. Doug and I looked back at the rhythm section and the four of us smiled in unison. Turning back to the audience, Doug, stepping forward with one foot on his floor monitor, laid out a sweet chord progression. Behind my stack of synthesizers, I answered Doug's phrases with right-handed organ fills and left-handed horn bursts.

Then Nancy, rocking her body back and forth to the beat, grabbed the microphone on the stand, closed her eyes, and belted out the first lyric of the song. Nancy's profile was exquisitely feminine and bore the almost angular beauty of an Egyptian queen. But her voice was deep and resonant and still able to reach notes in the higher register.

Midway through the song, I watched Doug prepare for his solo by tapping the electronic pedals at his feet, which allowed him to change the sound of his guitar. His solo soared over the other instruments and concluded with notes that sounded like a lover's cry.

The end of the solo signaled Nancy to sing the last verse with soulful urgency. Dancers, breathless but energized, sang along with her as she began the final chorus, with me and Doug adding tight harmony vocals above and below her voice.

When Denny ended the song with a powerful drum fill and cymbal crash, the audience gave us a commanding ovation. This feel continued all that night and over the next two nights.

Performing musicians often describe this experience as being *in the pocket.*

* * *

One night after playing, Nancy and Doug asked us if we wanted to swim in the heated outdoor pool next to the roadhouse parking lot.

None of us had any swimming apparel, and it was a chilly 38 degrees.

Doug, finishing rolling his cigarette, said with a sparkle in his eye, "Think of it like a poor man's jacuzzi."

With the guys wearing their boxers and Nancy dressed in something she'd converted into a body covering garment, we stepped out of our lodge robes and plunged into the steaming pool. With only our heads held above the water, the experience was akin to sitting in a hot tub and was quite pleasant.

As we talked and laughed about some of the things that had happened on our road trip, like the gun-toting manager and climbing into an unattended airplane, the experience felt like a ritual celebrating our bandhood.

It was then I decided to tell everyone about a movie I'd seen at one in the morning a week before we started our tour.

"So, there's this guy named George Bailey and he lives in this town called—I think it was Bedford Falls—where he runs his dad's building and loan business. Throughout the movie, he ends up helping everyone but himself. At one point, the Depression hits, the banks fail, and the townspeople stand to lose most of their savings . . . . " and on and on I went, telling my bandmates the entire plot of what is now a highly regarded film and a perennial favorite around Christmas. In 1983, It's a Wonderful Life was simply an obscure film in the public domain that had not yet been rediscovered.

Eventually, I got to the final third of the movie, continuing, "Uncle Billy's lost the $8,000, and Bailey, taking responsibility for the deficit, realizes it'll look like he embezzled the money, and he ends up thinking of killing himself."

Eric, slapping the steamy water in my direction, groaned and said, "Man, the whole thing sounds so depressing. This was a holiday movie? Crazy."

"Yeah, get to the finish line, Kev," said Doug.

"Hold on, I'm almost done. So, an angel named Clarence comes down to earth to show Bailey what things would have been like if he'd never been born. In the process, Clarence earns his wings."

Nancy laughed and said, "I can't believe you said that out loud."

Everybody laughed, including me because my narrative sounded patently absurd.

Denny, who had been silent the whole time, said, "I've seen it, too. Kev's spot-on. It's just better to see the flick. The whole thing with the angel is pretty cool—and funny."

About this time, we noticed the first few flakes of snow falling softy on the surface of the pool.

* * *

The midnight swimming episode is representative of the many times we bonded on and off stage. First, we respected each other as musicians. We'd had four changes in personnel early on, which only served to make us a tighter and more polished ensemble.

And, we all got along. Outside of work, our friendships blossomed through shared experiences like after-hours parties, going for coffee or a beer, Thanksgiving feasts, and going out to hear other bands (whom we regarded as the competition—some friendly, some not).

On this tour, Denny and I got particularly close riding in his small pickup with the camper shell. He shared stories about friends who owned exotic animals, like hawks, swans, reptiles, and ocean fish. He talked a lot about his family, particularly his father, who was a stylish, pipe-smoking fellow who enjoyed "taking it easy." Denny also shared his earliest musical experiences growing up in Oakland, California, being influenced by Black R&B musicians and getting an education in Motown and soul music. It helped explain how Denny was so well versed in different genres.

One night in Ruidoso, the band hung out in the roadhouse after hours and Denny taught me, Doug, and Eric how to do synchronized dance moves like the Temptations and Gladys Night & The Pips. We were amazed at how much Denny knew about these groups and their intricate choreography. It was pure joy learning how to do some simple moves to a rhythm Denny created by counting and clapping his hands.

On another occasion, Denny helped me tackle the funky clavinet riff in Stevie Wonder's masterpiece, "Superstition." I could pick out the notes that needed to be played, but I couldn't get the soulful feel of it. Denny knew exactly what I was missing. He said, "Don't play it like a piano; play it like you're playing drums with both hands. Make it percussive and funky."

He was so right.

Denny had another notable influence on me, and the rest of the band. He served as the bossy mother who reminded us when we needed to forego fast food and ultra-processed food and eat more nutritional meals. While in Ruidoso, Denny also coaxed us into trying escargot for the first time. It was okay, but sort of weird thinking that we were eating the very things we used to step on as kids after a good rain.

* * *

When our time in Ruidoso was up, the band was sad to be leaving the mountain lodge, with its rockin' roadhouse. The lush forests and clean mountain air were intoxicating, and we almost felt like we'd experienced a vacation in the wild. Now we had to return to Albuquerque to play four two-week gigs back to back.

On the morning we left, Eric surprised us as he produced an uncorked bottle of Chardonnay, which we passed around the van, except to Scott, who was driving. It symbolized a lift to our deflated mood as we took the long road home.

Back Home for a Time

Oct 3–Nov 26, 1983
Albuquerque Gigs

Thankfully, our management kept us on a continuous rotation through all the nightclubs that offered live music in Albuquerque, including Big Valley, Black Angus, Bogarts, Confetti, Friar's Pub, Friar's North, Friar's East, Graham Central Station, The Hungry Bear, Señor Buckets, and more.

Throughout our career, each engagement was typically a two-week affair, with the odd one-night stand here and there: We played a handful of school events, including some homecomings; a gig on the mall at The University of New Mexico; and once, in late 1980, an on-campus, beer-soaked fraternity party that—by comparison—made the movie Animal House look like an academic achievement documentary.

The Shakers also performed at several outdoor music festivals. For me, playing outside had its drawbacks: heat, sunlight glare, and acoustics. In a club, the sound reverberates and in essence is soaked up by the customers; outdoors, the sound of the instruments and vocals dissipates quickly in the air and wind.

Nov 28–Dec 9, 1983
Vacation/Rehearsal Time

Following a week-long vacation, we planned to hole up in our rehearsal space and learn some new songs. This included "New Song," by Howard Jones and "Wait Until Dark," which I'd written for the band.

Over the three-plus years the Shakers were together, we probably learned to play over 120 songs. On average, we'd play thirty-eight tunes each night in the clubs. But because the popularity of songs can diminish quickly, we'd have to constantly refresh our selection.

For musicians, learning to play an existing pop or rock record is a sure-fire way to train your ears to hear sometimes minute elements in a song. So, while all our band members could read music, it was quicker and more reliable for us to listen astutely to a song and deconstruct it in order to "cop" (or copy it).

Once each member of the band learned his or her part, we'd gather at the rehearsal space and play it together for the first time. Sometimes we'd have to tweak our parts to "correct" certain notes, chords, or lyrics. I can remember on one occasion when a five-minute argument broke out between Eric, Doug, and me over a single chord in a song. We couldn't agree on whether the chord was an E minor 9 or a G major 7!

Choosing which songs to play was another aspect of being a cover band. Each one of us contributed his or her own perspective on song selection.

For Nancy, the first criterion was, is it danceable? Another important contribution she made was occasionally recommending album cuts from hit records; the rationale? Since other Albuquerque bands would play the hits, why not select lesser known—but catchy—songs from the albums? Nancy also had an affinity for the Pretenders, the Divinyls, Joe Jackson, among many other artists.

Doug liked songs with cool chord progressions and catchy guitar riffs, but tired quickly of simply playing droning eighth-note rhythms throughout an entire song. To everyone's surprise, Doug turned out to be a really good singer—something he'd never done prior to being in the Shakers.

Eric had an impressive gift for pushing songs he knew our fans would like. Without his intuition, we'd have never learned "Hammer in My Heart," by Todd Rundgren or "Too Late," by the Shoes.

Naturally, I voted for songs with interesting keyboard parts, like the Producers' minor hit, "She Sheila." Further, I leaned toward songs with good harmony vocals, like "Magic," by the Cars or "Spirits in the Material World," by the Police.

Overall, Dennis rarely suggested songs, but always brought his A-game to whatever we decided to learn.

In my opinion, one of the coolest songs we ever covered was "To Sir, with Love," originally sung by Scottish singer, Lulu. Nancy, with acoustic guitar in hand, sang this song with heartfelt emotion, from soft elegance to ardent intensity. The band and the fans loved it.

Dec 12–Dec 24, 1983
Albuquerque Gig

Playing Christmas Eve was a surreal experience. At first, we'd feel sad for the collective loners who didn't appear to have anywhere else to be—with loved ones or with family. Then we'd chat with some and discover circumstances beyond our imagining: people whose connecting flights were cancelled due to weather; a doctor who was on call and drinking soda water and orange juice at her table; or dedicated loners who found quiet comfort in solitude to barricade themselves from the noise, commercialism, and chaos of the holidays.

This Christmas Eve felt a little like a rehearsal session, as we played the Pretender's "Middle of the Road" publicly for the first time. After playing it twice, we asked the twenty or so people in the bar which performance they thought sounded best.

The band left the club around 2:00 a.m. and drove to the Country Club neighborhood to see if the luminarias were still lit.

Like good Basque shepherds, we bundled up for the stroll and carried a Bota bag filled with brandy, which we passed around to keep warm. Someone's girlfriend—nice gal—asked several times if we were "having fun yet."

Jan 5–Feb 10, 1984
Albuquerque Gigs

One of the joys of being back in Albuquerque was getting to see so many in our fan base. Although we didn't know every Shakers follower by name, we always acknowledged them with a friendly nod or brief chat at their tables on our breaks.

We seemed to draw a diverse bunch of folks, from all walks of life. Shakers friends were journalists, dance instructors, actors, engineers, lawyers, construction workers, electricians, and more. They were ethnically diverse, straight, gay, married, and unmarried. They did have much in common: They were mostly good-natured people who loved to dance to music that was upbeat and fun.

Notably, more than a handful of couples met at Shaker gigs and married.

Best Band House and Blues Experiment

Feb 13–25, 1984
The Highlander Pub, Farmington

For the most part, the Farmington gig was a bust. The owners of the club were okay, the wait staff and bartenders were not unfriendly, but the place had no atmosphere—other than being a dark place for people to get drunk. This phenomenon was rare, but bands like the Shakers tried their best to avoid places that dampened their spirit and were simply a way to make money.

That said, the band house was ironically the best living quarters we'd had on the road, although its central furnace was not all that great. Thus, the kitchen became the center of activity, where late mornings we huddled around the Franklin stove, while Denny and Eric doubled up on making each of us a cup of coffee using the gas stove and a French press.

At the same time each morning, Scott brought firewood into the kitchen to keep the fire in the stove burning. Though I've said little about him, Scott was a gentle giant of a man. We'd always considered him part of the band, but he tended to keep to himself, unless we planned an activity he found interesting. At work, he did a marvelous job of setting up and running our sound system for the better part of two years.

Behind the mixing console, Scott set all the volume levels of our microphones, guitars, keyboards, and drums. He adjusted the "sound" we desired for each instrument or mic, using a host of tools, like equalizers to set low-, mid-, and high-frequency levels and effects processors, such as echo and reverb, to enhance the color of the sound.

Scott was generally a quiet fellow with a wry sense of humor, but he had the heft and muscle to protect us in sometimes risky bar environments. And, he made a mean batch of posole.

Scott all but adopted a pit bull, owned by the property manager in the Farmington band house, that followed him everywhere he went. Scott never knew the dog's official moniker, but after a few days of calling him Bo, the dog responded accordingly.

* * *

I recall the morning we all crowded into the kitchen to watch the 1984 Winter Olympics in Sarajevo, Yugoslavia. We tuned in right when the women's singles figure skating competition was underway.

"Oh man! Perfect double-axel!" yelled Doug at the small black and white TV on the kitchen counter. "Germany's a shoo-in on technical merit."

"No way, dude; the U.S. skater executed three triple jumps!" Denny countered.

"Yeah, but she landed roughly on that third jump . . . . Woah! A triple toe loop!" Doug yelled again at the TV.

(I kept wondering how they knew all these figure skating moves.)

"Well I'm still rooting for the American," said Denny.

"Your choice," Doug concluded. "I admire the athleticism of the skaters, no matter which country they represent."

It turned out that Doug was right, when East Germany's Katarina Witt took the gold.

After a time, Nancy and I decided to go for a short walk. It was a crisp winter morning, but the view from the backyard was picturesque, with beautiful homes stretching along the high banks of the Animas River. Against a cloudless blue sky, Sandhill Cranes flew over us in a V formation.

"It's a pretty nice town," Nancy offered. "I just wish the club we're playing at was better."

"No kidding, Nance."

"I've been meaning to ask you something," Nancy said softly. "I wondered why you never asked more about why Doug and I split up."

It was a somber subject, to be sure. Nancy and Doug had been married for years, but had announced their pending divorce before we went on tour.

"I'm really sorry about not sayin' much," I said. "It's that I love both you guys and didn't wanna take sides, you know."

"We didn't expect you to take sides. Our decision was mutual."

"Then, what happened?"

"It was too much togetherness, I guess. Living and working together did us in. At home we started to feel like we were just roommates," she said.

I didn't reply, so Nancy broke the silence. "I hope you'll talk to Doug, Kevin. He may have a different perspective than I. But—like me—I think it hit him pretty hard."

"Will do."

I was witnessing firsthand one of the perils of married couples playing together in a band.

* * *

As I said previously, the Farmington bar didn't have much character. We did have four or five good nights over the two weeks, when the place was at capacity; and—while the audience wasn't very responsive—they did dance sluggishly to our high-energy music. Apparently, New Wave wasn't their thing.

Some drama did ensue on a slow Tuesday night when we played to eight people, not counting the flies sitting at the bar. Nancy, usually a fount of charisma, became visibly bored and, turning to face the band, said "Let's drop the Cyndi Lauper tune and do a slow blues number in E."

The band was game, so Denny counted off a slow 1-2-3-4, and Doug laid down a bluesy guitar intro, then nodded at Nancy, who started to sing some soulful blues lyrics, improvised completely on the fly:

It's a ca-vern, not a ta-vern
A wa-tering hole, and a car-nival show
High-lander . . . You're bringin' me down
'Scuse me if I slan-der . . . High-lan-der
Yeah, you're bringin' me down.

Nancy got through two more verses, when our eyes were drawn to the back of the bar.

The manager of the Highlander Pub was not amused. As with the manger in Los Lunas, he summoned us to his office to be lectured on our criticism of his bar.

"What's all this about? I'm paying you guys to entertain our customers, not trash our establishment!" he said with a scowl.

Doug decided on the spot to take charge of the situation.

"Mr. Wilkins, we didn't mean to put your club down. Actually, we were just doing what any rock band worth its salt should be able to do, which is—"

Nancy finished Doug's thought, "—play the blues."

Wilkins turned his attention to Nancy as she continued, "We were following the tradition of blues artists like Billie Holiday, Aretha Franklin, B.B. King, and—"

"Yeah, but you were putting us down!" he interrupted.

Doug waved the olive branch by summing up, "Mr. Wilkins—Matt—sorry about playing a blues number you found offensive. It won't happen again."

The blues incident, as it came to be called by the band, punctuated our time at the Highlander Pub.

The Band's on Fire When Fate Deals Us a Card—Face Down

Feb 27–Mar 10, 1984
Ely's Roadhouse, Las Cruces

The week beginning February 27 was to test our mojo when it came to being the best we could be as professional musicians.

The easiest way to describe Ely's Roadhouse is to picture a cavernous barn, with high ceilings, visible ceiling beams and joists, rustic wood floors (except the dance floor), a long bar, an adjacent pool room, and a parking lot filled with Harley-Davidson motorcycles. On any given night you might see a minivan or two displaying pictures of lovers silhouetted against a fluorescent sunset.

And if Ely's was a big barn, then the Shakers were going to put on a show—and we did. With a week's vacation following this last tour stop, the band really wanted to blow it out as hard as we could.

We'd played biker bars before, like New Mexico's Golden Inn, and knew that we'd be getting requests to play the Doobie Brothers, Rolling Stones, Lynyrd Skynyrd, and music by other meat-and-potatoes rock bands, but what saved us was the willingness of the biker gals to dance to whatever we played, as long as it had a strong beat. This prompted the guys to join the party.

And after all, the Shakers were a dance band. Because we attracted people who loved to trip the light fantastic, we seldom encountered troublemakers—even in some of the rougher bars where we played.

* * *

On Wednesday night, Nancy looked great in a short skirt, boots, neck scarf, and sparkling bracelets as she joined us on stage. After two good sets, we began the third set with a popular song titled, "99 Luftballons (99 Red Balloons)," by the German rock band, Nena. Because the lyrics were sung in German, and Nancy didn't speak it, she memorized and sang the words phonetically. It was a risky thing to do, but she was vindicated when a language professor at the University of New Mexico confirmed that her pronunciation was 82% correct, even though none of us knew what the song was about. (An English language version of the song was quickly released after the German version charted at #2 on the US Billboard Hot 100. Ironically, the German singer sounded like she was singing English phonetically!)

Beginning the song with a hymn-like, organ and string part, I watched the dancers watching us to see what was coming next. Over this wave of sound, Nancy sang the first verse, the end of which signaled me to strike the keys on my synthesizer—creating a thundering bass line. Locked in rhythm with Dennis' drums, I looked at Doug and Eric across the stage and smiled as the whole band joined in and shook the rafters in the barn.

But the song belonged to Nancy, whose voice carried the obscure lyric passionately over the giant cavern of the club—her body swaying to the music with an army of dancers pressed against the stage.

When the song came to its dramatic conclusion and I sent the pitch of the last note on my synthesizer three octaves higher in a smooth arc (called a glissando), Nancy stepped back as the club patrons clapped vigorously and said,

"Danke . . . . . . That's 'thanks' in German!" To which the crowd laughed and clapped even harder.

The remainder of the set—in fact, the entire evening—went exceedingly well.

Other highlights included our covers of "Back on the Chain Gang," a jangly Pretenders tune that prompted couples to do some slower western dancing, and the up-tempo "One Thing Leads to Another," by the FIXX. The middle section of the latter song had an instrumental break in which Dennis played a pounding groove on the drums as he shouted to the band:

"Hey band!"

"Yeah! (Eric and Doug yelling into one microphone.)

"Are we gonna get down tonight?"

"Yeah!"

"We gonna party tonight?"

"Yeah!"

Moments after, Eric played a riveting and technically accomplished bass solo that sent his fingers up and down the neck of the instrument. In perfect step with the drums, Eric slapped the strings on his instrument aggressively, his mouth wide open as if reacting to his own technique.

Doug's clear, ringing guitar came up at the end of Eric's solo, ushering in the rest of the song with a wave of melodic chords for Nancy to sing over.

The final set of the evening allowed me to play my guitar on another crowd pleaser: Johnny Rivers' "Secret Agent Man."

We always started the song with the guitars playing the repeating riff of Henry Mancini's "Peter Gunn" theme, which then segued into the similar but distinctively twangy Secret Agent riff. I got to sing lead on this song, drawing strength all the way from my toes to my vocal cords. Notably, Doug achieved some sleight-of-hand by dropping in a piece of the "James Bond Theme" in a guitar fill between lines in the verses. The tune always brought the house down and was a good number to dance to.

Doug and Nancy were featured prominently on the final song of the night, with a tune that, to the patrons in the club, probably felt like four minutes of music crammed into two minutes and thirty seconds. "Breathless," by the punk rock band X, gave Doug and Nancy the opportunity to demonstrate their tight vocalization that was reminiscent of the "Alphabet Song" sung four times faster than a class of first graders.

Doug and I strummed our electric guitars as fast as we could to create a foundation over which the lyrics could fly. The tune also gave Doug a chance to play a raw and wickedly fast solo that seemed inspired by Chuck Berry and Keith Richards, but which he made entirely his own.

Looking out into the crowd, it became clear to us that the customers didn't know what to make of this type of song, as they stood and watched silently for the song and the set to come to an end.

* * *

As the week progressed, we began to see more and more non-biker patrons, who formed an eclectic group of "Las Crucens." We learned that word had gotten 'round that Ely's had a killer dance band with a dynamic red-headed singer.

Then, catching all of us off guard, Nancy called us all together after Friday's last set and startled us with the news that she was beginning to lose her voice.

Sitting on the edge of the stage, she explained what was happening.

"Something doesn't feel right with my vocal cords," she said, delicately touching the base of her neck.

"It's not like it hurts, exactly . . . it just feels like somethings off." Looking at the rest of us standing in a semicircle around her, she could read the concern on our faces.

Eric spoke first, "Wow, Nance . . . Do you think you can sing tomorrow night? If you can, at least we could fulfill part of our two-week contract. Our manager could maybe send a replacement band that's on his roster."

Looking quite serious, Nancy returned, "I think I can do Saturday night, but after that—well my throat doctor would surely instruct me to stop singing so I don't do any permanent damage."

Doug, easing the tension of the moment, said, "Hey, I'll lay odds that Cruces has some live bands, maybe with a female singer. We could coach her during the day and have her fronting the band at night. Let's ask the staff if they know anyone."

After a series of impromptu meetings with the bar manager and staff, one of the bartenders wrote down the name and number of a local singer in a New Wave band.

* * *

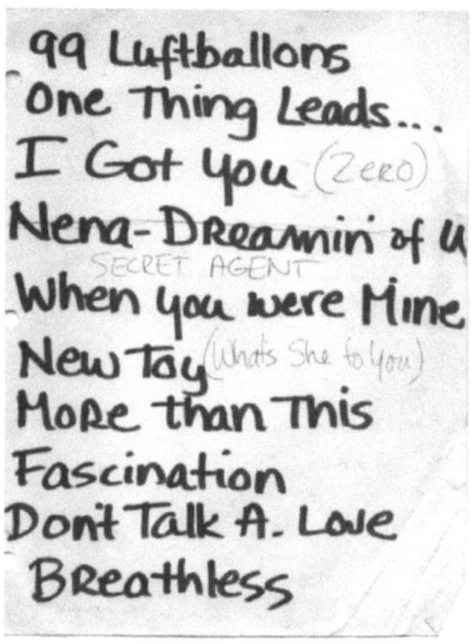

Sitting across from me, Doug, and Nancy at Ely's, Nikki Bridges—all five feet, three inches of her—looked a little like petite singer Pat Benatar, with her short, dark hair; pursed lips; and small nose. We learned quickly that she sang with Nikki's Rangers and that she knew at least eighteen of the thirty-five songs on our set lists. We told her that the Shakers could repeat some tunes and lengthen guitar and keyboard solos each night to make up for a shorter set list; we added that it might be necessary for her to read some lyrics from a notebook we'd provide to her.

Nikki spoke in a disarmingly soft voice that made us worry about her vocal strength, but we didn't have any other options.

"I can do this. I just need to study the songs and have someone give me cues for when to come in and when to stop," she said in a business-like manner.

I was elected to serve in that role because we didn't want Nancy to have to use her voice at all during the second week at Ely's. And Doug made it official by offering to pay Nikki a generous salary if she could commit to this rescue gig. (Doug and I were glad that Nancy looked relieved after this meeting. This predicament had never happened before, and we all felt for her.)

Nancy, always the professional, delivered Saturday night by singing all four sets, if holding back a bit of intensity to protect her voice. We also avoided the songs requiring what we called "vocal gymnastics." Despite these small changes, the dancers and drinkers all seemed fully engaged.

* * *

I spent most of Sunday going over our song list with Nikki, giving her as much coaching as possible to help her navigate the songs' arrangements. Thankfully, soundman Scott frequently recorded our performances on cassettes to help us gauge how well we sounded; these tapes became indispensable to Nikki.

Then, Monday and Tuesday morning, the band showed up early at Ely's and conducted rehearsals with our stand-in singer. We then went to work Tuesday night, and the die was cast.

The Shakers took the stage at 8:30. We all huddled together around Nikki, and Doug told her in his matter-of-fact voice, "You've got this!" and smiled.

Doug announced our guest vocalist from Nikki's Rangers to the audience, and Dennis counted off the first song.

Nikki was dressed in a black vest with silver buttons, a short skirt, and black boots with heels that bumped her height up several inches. She sang "Mission of Mercy," by the

Motels, with a solid delivery and good pitch, and by the third set, she started to gel pretty well with the band.

Perhaps because of nerves and hyper-concentration, Nikki planted her feet on the stage and faced the dance floor with little facial expression or body motion. Her serious demeanor gave off a clear message, as if to say, "Don't bug me—I'm workin' here!" It wasn't ego; rather, it reflected her resolve for doing the best she could.

But by Thursday night, Nikki seemed more relaxed. She continued to look at me for cues when Doug or I were going to do a solo or we were going to repeat a chorus. I got pretty good at mouthing words broadly at her for her cues.

* * *

During each day, the band briefly touched base with Nancy, who stayed close to the band house, making her own meals, drinking herbal teas, and practicing other things her throat doctor had recommended for healing inflamed vocal cords.

On Friday morning, Nancy surprised us all when she told us during lunch that she really felt like she could sing Saturday night. She'd had a long-distance phone call to her doctor, who trusted Nancy's intuition about singing the final night of our gig—and our tour.

Doug notified Nikki of the revised plan, but asked her if she'd be at the club Saturday night as a safety net in case Nancy ran into problems. (She would still be paid for the last night, whether she sang or not.) Nikki was very cool with the request and said she'd bring her entire band to the roadhouse Saturday because they'd heard so many good things about Nancy and the Shakers.

Minutes before Saturday's showtime, Nancy, in her signature fiesta dress, boots, and black hat, stood on the stage facing our drummer—the two of them laughing about something or other, as Dennis did a "tah-dump-ting" on the snare and cymbal as if responding to a funny story. For the first time that week, everyone in the band felt a sense of relief and anticipation that we could end the week in a blaze of glory.

No doubt aided by a boost of adrenaline and determination, Nancy led the band through a rousing rendition of "Burning Down the House," by the Talking Heads. Right away, people headed for the dance floor, ready to cut loose. More than once this night, Nancy looked at each of us on the stage with a knowing smile that said we were back.

Highlights of the night included Joe Jackson's "I'm the Man," with Eric's string-bending bass technique, Dennis' driving beat, and Nancy's swishing skirt dance moves; the Pretenders' "Middle of the Road," featuring Doug's shimmering guitar and bluesy harmonica solo; and Men Without Hats' minimalist pop tune, "Safety Dance," where I got to play some whimsical passages on my three synthesizers.

Just before the third set, the bar was completely packed, and we were told by a waitress that some people were waiting to get in. She also told us that "the vibe was so good, all the mean people and druggies had to go outside."

We also noticed that Nikki and her bandmates had made it to the club and had a table near the dance floor. Doug and I stepped over to their table for introductions and to again thank Nikki for helping us out this past week.

In sets three and four, we got to play some of the songs I'd written for the band, which were popular with our Albuquerque fans. This included our most requested original, "Don't Talk About Love," a rock duet I'd written where Nancy and I sang the melody and harmony through the entire song:

What's that you said?
It caught me off guard
Came without warning
Gave me a start

'Scuse my reaction
It's so hard to conceal
Cause you never tell me – no, no, no
The way that you feel

But just how else was I supposed to know?
Why can't I feel it when I touch you?
Even in love you're in complete control and far away

Don't talk about love to me
It isn't fair to lead me on – no, no, no
Don't talk about love to me
When all we do is get it on

Toward the end of the final set, Nancy stepped up to the microphone for an announcement and—motioning toward Nikki's table—said, "Some of you may realize that we had some help this week from one of Las Cruces' own: Nikki Bridges, of Nikki's Rangers."

A good many people in the audience shouted a "wooooo-hooooo" cheer and clapped for the local musicians.

"I'd like to invite Nikki to come sing a tune with us." Sweeping her arm across the dance floor, she added, "What do you think?"

Again, the crowd erupted in cheers.

Nikki looked legitimately surprised by Nancy's invitation. In fact, our band was, too, but we were totally good with it. Dennis yelled out, "Hell yeah!"

When Nikki joined us on stage, we motioned for her to use Doug's mic. Nancy stepped over to the singer and said, "How about 'Girls Just Want to Have Fun?' Let's trade verses and vamp our way through the ride-out," which meant—let's improvise the repeating chorus at the end and do a call and response between us.

Dennis counted off the first beats of Cyndi Lauper's hit single, and away we went. The dance floor filled up again, and the dancers watched the two vocalists lay it down.

Both Nancy and Nikki moved their bodies to the beat as the song progressed, with each taking a verse and then one covering the melody, the other covering the harmony on the choruses.

At the ride-out, each singer answered what kind of fun they'd like to have while the band sang "Girls, they wanna, they wanna have fun—girls—they wanna have—"

Their humorous responses ranged from "frozen-lobe drinks," to "a boyfriend who cooks," to "a Stingray sports car," and more.

The level of excitement was palpable as the band finished the song and Nikki rejoined her bandmates. Nancy thanked her again for standing in for her during the week. She then motioned toward Scott at the mixing console on the far side of the dance floor and thanked him for "making us sound good every night! Beam me up, Scotty!"

The Shakers typically ended the night with a raucous punk-based tune by the Pretenders, called "The Wait"—a tradition we preserved at Ely's Roadhouse.

Starting with a grungy, distorted guitar intro, Doug and I strummed our guitars at a furious tempo as Nancy sang the razor-sharp lyrics, which sounded like streams of distress for the forgotten urban child.

In the middle section of the song, the instruments began an urgent, percussive "chunk-ka, chunk-ka, chunk-ka, chunk-ka" sound with Doug, Eric, and me lined up with our guitars side by side, like three swashbuckling swordsmen.

By this time, the dancers—moving frenetically to the beat—seemed to be watching for what the band would do next.

At this moment, Nancy started to talk to the audience:

"Okay, okay, you guys look great . . . . . Shall we do it? . . . . .Yeah, let's do it! . . . . Okay—everybody down . . . . . down on the ground. That's right! On your backs. All the way down."

Two thirds of the dancers were game, and they adjusted their pants or skirts to lay on their backs on the dance floor.

Nancy then continued, "Okay, everybody wiggle . . . . . That's it! . . . . Wiggle!"

The dance floor became a sea of legs moving back and forth that reminded me of swimmers kicking their legs in a pool.

"You guys look great," shouted Nancy. "Okay, everybody stand up . . . . . Give yourself a round of applause."

Back on their feet, the dancers continued their workout as Doug charged into a wild guitar solo. When Nancy came back for the last verse, Eric and Doug were playing back to back like two bookends, which added to the spectacle.

After a long crescendo, the song ended with two quick power chords, to which the dancers applauded and hollered.

We were jazzed to see so many bikers and others in the place holding up their lighters and whistling. Unfortunately, we'd played a longer set than usual and we couldn't do the encore requested by the audience.

Ending our set at 1:00 a.m., the band accepted Nikki Bridges' invitation to join a party at the Rangers' rehearsal house. But truth be told, we were all pretty well spent, having pivoted quickly to an unforeseen event and having played full time since early December. What we were really looking forward to was a week off to refuel and allow Nancy's voice to rest.

When giving Nikki our goodbyes, the singer rather stiffly hugged and kissed me, I think because of our prep together and my onstage directions. It was a sweet recognition from a fellow musician, and everyone in the band made sure to give me a hard time about it!

On March 11, we collected all our gear and set our sights on home; Albuquerque was 230 miles away.

* * *

The Shakers continued to perform through 1984, but did fewer out-of-town gigs. We'd become so popular in Albuquerque that we had to let our manager know when to schedule time off for us.

During this period, one of our favorite places to play was Graham Central Station, a spacious venue for major-label acts. It was here that we opened for the Motels, Leon Russell, and Ricky Nelson. We were also booked to open for Men at Work, until the Australian band switched to bigger venues in response to their mega hit singles, "Down Under" and "Who Can it Be Now?"

Roaring Toward the Finish Line

Late in 1984, Nancy, Doug, and I began to consider disbanding the Shakers. We loved playing music but had become weary of "bar band" life. Essentially, being a working musician meant being out of sync with the "Five O'clock World." And personally, I tired of the smoky, perpetually dark, and stale atmosphere of bars.

We weren't surprised that the Shakers' rhythm section was interested in joining other local bands, while the rest of us set our sights on different ambitions. Nancy and Doug were planning a move to New York City, a music mecca where they could play their own music and possibly gain the attention of a record label. And I wanted to pursue a career as a songwriter, penning songs for established artists.

Our final gig was on September 30, 1984 at Confetti—a nightclub that could accommodate hundreds of patrons. The night of the concert, the club was packed to the rafters, with a long line of people waiting outside to get in. We were fortunate to have videographer/audio engineer, John Cline, and soundman, Phil Appelbaum, videotape this last Shakers' performance. As a stroke of genius, John elected to shoot the video right on stage, to give viewers the experience of playing in the band. Christened The Shakers, Last Tango, the video can be viewed at the YouTube link on page 41.

The video was a perfect swansong to a band that Nancy, Doug, Eric, Dennis, and I loved dearly, and I wouldn't change the experiences we had for anything.

Today, I'm always delighted when, every now and then, a fan of the band catches my attention and says something like, "Hey man, weren't those good times? Are you still in touch with your bandmates?"

Just last year, an old fan stepped up to me in an automotive repair shop and asked with a smile,

"What's Shakin?"

About the Band

Origin of the Band's Name

When I joined Doug and Nancy's band, it was called The Authorities. Though not a bad name, it did sound a bit too much like The Police, who were gaining popularity with their hits "Message in a Bottle" and "Walking on the Moon." After mustering some courage, I suggested changing our name to The Shakers, as it conjured up images of people dancing with abandon or grooving to a pulsating beat. The band voted on it, and that became our new moniker. We were, after all, a dance band.

It interested me too that there was a New England communal sect called the Shakers, who believed in women's equality, were largely considered pacifists, danced wildly during religious ceremonies, and are known for their furniture-making.

Here is our original logo:

Band Biographies

Nancy Howell (lead vocals, rhythm guitar, percussion)
G. Douglas Pierson (lead guitar, harmonica, vocals)
Kevin Hughes (keyboards, rhythm guitar, vocals)
Eric Benjamin (bass, vocals)
Dennis Painter (drums, percussion, vocals)

Nancy Howell was voted "girl most likely to succeed" in high school, and the nominating committee was apparently correct. As a young person, she had been strongly influenced by her older brother, Gary, who'd been in bands by the time he was in his teens. A confirmed Beatle fanatic, Nancy learned her craft listening and singing to rock standards in her bedroom, until she was confident she could pursue a career as a rock vocalist. Nancy was also a fine artist, creating striking stained-glass art and perfecting the art of calligraphy. She considered herself a joiner, which to me meant she was outgoing and interested in collaboration. As a singer with the Shakers, Albuquerque audiences loved her. As a charismatic performer, there was no one better.

Today, Nancy paints in oils and creates stop-motion animated videos with her husband, Mark Lerner.

Doug Pierson let his guitar and harmonica do the talking. A man of few words, Doug rolled his own cigarettes, did carpentry work on the side, and was a general handyman capable of fixing pretty much anything in the home. His father, who had climbed some of the highest peaks in the Andes mountain range, was a bona fide world adventurer—something Doug would aspire to in his own life—circumnavigating the world in a sailboat. In the Shakers, Doug demonstrated an organic feel for the electric guitar. His rhythm guitar playing was solid and inventive, and his solos and guitar fills were melodic or raucous when they needed to be. He was also able to sing French lyrics expertly—which became necessary on several songs.

Doug and Nancy had been married before the Shakers formed in 1980. In 1984, even though they were divorced, the two journeyed together to New York City (NYC) to form a band called Clovis Noches (Clovis Nights). After a few years, Nancy met (and married) Mark Lerner and joined his band, Flat Old World—a popular eight-piece band that played backwoods music at a glacial pace. She sang and played guitar, and Doug played concertina and tuba.

After Clovis Noches disbanded, Doug became an environmental consultant for a large engineering firm. He continues to play music and is now in several NYC bands, including The Highland Shatners, Lasso Mary, and a band that performs in Harlem called the SugarHillBillys. Doug particularly enjoyed one music project called Waterways, which was a collection of original songs about NYC's waterways (below).

I, **Kevin Hughes**, was keyboardist and rhythm guitar player, harmony vocalist, and principal songwriter for the Shakers. Though I'd been a happy hour, folk-rock singer during college, I warmed quickly to the idea of playing the high-energy, percolating pop-rock of New Wave, which was born out of the punk movement. Using my three synthesizers, I could play piano, organ, horn, string, and percussive parts that sounded remarkably like the real instruments. I also sang lead on a handful of songs to give Nancy a breather and often sang high harmonies above Nancy's lead vocals, which helped me forge a strong falsetto vocal technique.

But my greatest thrill was writing songs for Nancy to sing and the band to play. To do this successfully, I endeavored to capture her vocal style and persona. For example, as Nancy's star power started to become a burden, she used to hide behind sunglasses or sit under my piano during our band breaks. My song, "Hide Me," expressed her frame of mind:

I give up—take me away
Drive me to the house on a hill
Let me alone, leave me in the garden
I could run but I never will

You work so hard to be the center of attention
Thank the ones too numerous to mention
Turn around and you find you need to be alone

Can you hide me, do you know a place where no-one ever goes?
If you like me, we could hide together
Who will ever know?

Following the Shakers, I became a senior instructional designer and video script writer and director for a technical services firm. Between 2007 and 2024, I played baby boomer music in a duo with guitarist/singer, Joe DeBonis. We played covers from the 60s and 70s and our own compositions.

Eric Benjamin (a.k.a. Eric Been Jammin') was a little bit crazy and a little bit reckless, but he was a phenomenal bass player in the Shakers. He was also one of the reasons fans came to watch the band play. On stage, Eric yelled and screamed at all the opportune times as if to order the band to charge ahead or to pull out all the stops. He sometimes smiled broadly, sometimes he winced as if he was in pain, while other times he closed his eyes and dug deep into the rhythm of a song with our drummer, Dennis. Though I knew little of him prior to joining the band, I know that he was working in a camera shop when he joined the Shakers.

At one point in our band history, some rival musicians coaxed Eric to leave the Shakers and play bass in their new band. Once the secret was disclosed, Nancy, more than anyone, convinced Eric that he was cherished by all the members of the Shakers and that he would be walking away from the most popular band in Albuquerque to join another band with an uncertain future. Fortunately, she was successful, and Eric stayed with the Shakers until the band's break-up in 1984.

Sometime later, Eric moved to Chicago, where he worked for Cenflo Inc., a publisher of trade journals in the floral and nursery industries owned by his father. Returning to New Mexico in 2004, Eric died in 2010, at the age of 51.

Dennis Painter was a professional drummer long before being invited to join the Shakers. Denny had played in working bands in Oakland, California and in popular Albuquerque bands. In addition to his skill, he provided us with an education about the music business, including the dangers of signing contracts that could paralyze a working band for years. But he knew we needed to align ourselves with booking agents that could keep us working full time. On stage, he also knew how to keep people on the dance floor by melding one tune into the next, which club owners loved because it made customers thirsty.

After the Shakers disbanded, Denny worked for several decades in a very popular rock and blues band called Harvey and the Prowlers. Dennis died in January 2026, at the age of 72.

Links to Shakers Media

The Shakers, Last Tango video (recorded at Confetti, in front of hundreds of fans):

https://www.youtube.com/watch?v=evUt2S0m210

The Shakers' music video, plus live performance on TV:

Our band had won a battle-of-the-bands competition and funds to make a very, very low-budget music video. So, we drove out East Central to the Western Skies Hotel—a crumbling and downright ghostly lodge whose heyday had long since passed. There, we hauled lights, camera equipment, and props (including a rotary telephone and a dismembered mannequin) up a circular staircase to a remote room in the complex. We scoped out the room, with its mottled shag carpet, black tuck and roll furniture, and funky bathroom fixtures.

JFK, Marilyn Monroe, and probably Abe Lincoln were known to have stayed there, but the place was now barely operational and serviced by a skeleton crew of young people who seemed happy to have our company. We never encountered any other guests.

If I didn't know better, I'd swear that the Eagles' most famous song was written expressly for this sad and creepy establishment. Still, it served us well for our cheesy video and we were able to both check out and leave.

You'll notice in the video that you can barely make out any images because the producer used old ¾-inch videotape that had probably been recycled a dozen times before his crew shot our video. Nancy much preferred the live concert video that begins at 3:45.

https://www.youtube.com/watch?v=YltZElJEfNA

Kevin Hughes: Shake Your Memory CD:

This album comprises personal re-recordings of some of the songs I wrote for the Shakers. During our four-year run, I composed and arranged most of the band's original songs, which I crafted for our lead singer, Nancy Howell.

https://kevinhughes.bandcamp.com/album/shake-your-memory

About the Author

Kevin Hughes is a lifelong native of Albuquerque, New Mexico, where he lives with his wife, Mary. Since earning his bachelor's degree in English in 1979, he has been a professional musician, composer and songwriter, technical writer, instructional designer, and video producer and director.

As a writer, Kevin favors the short-story form, which can reveal truths through life-changing events occurring within a brief moment in time. An admirer of the works of O. Henry, Shirley Jackson, John Updike, and Anthony Doerr, Kevin has published two works of fiction: *Salvage: Short and Shorter Stories*, and *Connections and Other Stories*.

Kevin's first work of non-fiction—*Making Music with the Shakers*—chronicles his experience as a member of Albuquerque's most popular New Wave rock band, active in the early 1980s. His colorful narrative explores the life of a working musician; the creative process for writing, learning, and playing songs; the joys and pitfalls of this lifestyle; and the often-humorous episodes that occurred as the band toured New Mexico nightclubs and roadhouses.

The book closes with biographies of the five band members and provides links to live Shakers performance videos, as well as recordings of songs Kevin composed for the quintet.

www.ingramcontent.com/pod-product-compliance
Lightning Source LLC
LaVergne TN
LVHW070151110826
845147LV00002B/371

9798234066459